DEDICATION

To those who dare to dream of a future powered by intelligent machines. May this book be your compass in navigating the exciting world of AI implementation.

Revolutionize Your Business with AI

A Step-by-Step Guide

Benjamin Evans

Copyright © 2024 Benjamin Evans

All rights reserved.

CONTENTS

ACKNOWLEDGMENTS 1
CHAPTER 1 1
Introduction to AI Solutions 1
    1.1 What is Artificial Intelligence (AI)? 1
    1.2 Demystifying AI: Core Concepts and Technologies 3
    1.3 The Rise of AI Solutions: Transforming Industries 5
CHAPTER 2 7
Identifying Business Needs for AI 7
    2.1 Evaluating Your Business Landscape 7
    2.2 Defining Problems and Opportunities for AI Integration 10
    2.3 Aligning AI Solutions with Business Goals 15
CHAPTER 3 18
Understanding AI Applications Across Industries 18
    3.1 AI in Customer Service and Marketing 18
    3.2 AI in Manufacturing and Supply Chain Management 20
    3.3 AI in Healthcare and Life Sciences 22
    3.4 AI in Other Industries 27
CHAPTER 4 30
Planning and Design for AI Implementation 30
    4.1 Defining Project Scope and Success Metrics 30
    4.2 Choosing the Right AI Approach (Machine Learning, Deep Learning etc.) 33
    4.3 Data Acquisition and Preparation for AI Models 37
CHAPTER 5 40
Building and Training AI Models 40
    5.1 Selecting AI Tools and Platforms 40
    5.2 Training Data Management and Optimization 43
    5.3 Model Training, Evaluation, and Refinement 44
CHAPTER 6 47
Integrating AI Solutions into Existing Systems 47
    6.1 Data Pipelines and Infrastructure Development 47

6.2 User Interface and User Experience Design for AI Integration 48

6.3 Change Management and User Adoption Strategies...............50

6.4 Monitoring and Maintaining AI Models....................................51

CHAPTER 7.. 53

Testing and Deployment of AI Solutions... 53

7.1 Performance Testing and Benchmarking................................. 53

7.2 Security Considerations and Ethical Implications of AI............ 54

7.3 Deployment Strategies and Monitoring Processes.................. 56

CHAPTER 8.. 58

Evaluating and Maintaining AI Systems..58

8.1 Monitoring AI Performance and Model Drift...........................58

8.2 Continuous Improvement and Model Retraining.................... 59

8.3 Explainability and Transparency in AI Decisions...................... 61

CHAPTER 9.. 63

The Future of AI: Trends and Advancements..63

9.1 Emerging AI Technologies and Applications............................ 63

9.2 The Impact of AI on Jobs and the Workforce..........................66

9.3 Responsible AI Development and Governance........................67

CHAPTER 10.. 69

Conclusion: A Roadmap to AI Success... 69

10.1 Key Takeaways for Implementing AI Solutions.......................69

10.2 Building an AI-Ready Organization..71

10.3 The Journey Continues: A Look Ahead.................................... 72

ABOUT THE AUTHOR.. 75

ACKNOWLEDGMENTS

This book wouldn't have been possible without the support and contributions of many incredible individuals.

First and foremost, my deepest gratitude goes to the countless researchers, developers, and innovators who have dedicated their careers to pushing the boundaries of Artificial Intelligence. Their tireless work has laid the foundation upon which this book, and the future of AI, is built.

A special thanks to my mentors and colleagues who have provided invaluable guidance and feedback throughout this journey. Their insights and expertise have been instrumental in shaping the content and direction of this book.

I am also grateful to the reviewers who offered their time and expertise to ensure the accuracy and clarity of the information presented. Your critical feedback has been essential in making this book a valuable resource.

Finally, my heartfelt appreciation goes to my family and friends for their unwavering support and encouragement. Your patience and understanding have allowed me to dedicate the time and energy necessary to bring this book to life.

Thank you all.

CHAPTER 1

INTRODUCTION TO AI SOLUTIONS

Artificial intelligence (AI) has become a ubiquitous term, woven into headlines, boardroom discussions, and even casual conversation. But what exactly is AI, and how is it translating from science fiction to real-world applications? This chapter serves as your launchpad into the exciting world of AI solutions, demystifying its core concepts, exploring its underlying technologies, and showcasing its transformative impact across industries.

1.1 What is Artificial Intelligence (AI)?

At its core, AI refers to the ability of machines to mimic human cognitive functions like learning, problem-solving, and decision-making. However, unlike the simplistic robots of our past, AI systems don't rely on pre-programmed instructions. Instead, they leverage sophisticated algorithms and vast amounts of data to continuously learn and improve their performance.

Key characteristics of AI:

- **Learning:** AI systems can learn from data without explicit programming. This allows them to adapt to new situations and improve their performance over time. Machine learning and deep learning are two prominent techniques used to achieve this capability.
- **Reasoning:** AI systems can analyze and process information to draw conclusions and make decisions. This can involve logical reasoning, probabilistic analysis, and even forms of common-sense reasoning.
- **Problem-solving:** AI systems can identify problems, develop solutions, and take actions to achieve desired outcomes. This can involve planning, searching, and optimization techniques.

Differentiating AI from Automation:

It's important to distinguish AI from automation. Automation refers to the use of technology to perform repetitive tasks without human intervention. While automation can be a component of AI solutions, it's not the defining characteristic. AI systems go beyond automating tasks; they can learn, adapt, and solve problems independently.

1.2 Demystifying AI: Core Concepts and Technologies

Understanding some fundamental concepts and technologies is crucial to grasp the power of AI:

- **Machine Learning (ML):** This subfield of AI focuses on algorithms that learn from data. By analyzing large datasets, ML algorithms can identify patterns, make predictions, and improve their performance without explicit programming. Common ML techniques include decision trees, support vector machines, and neural networks.

- **Deep Learning:** A subset of ML inspired by the structure and function of the human brain. Deep learning algorithms consist of artificial neural networks with multiple layers, allowing them to process complex information and learn intricate patterns from massive datasets. This is particularly powerful for tasks like image recognition, natural language processing, and speech recognition.

- **Data:** The fuel that powers AI. AI systems rely on vast amounts of data to learn and improve. The quality and quantity of data significantly impact the performance and effectiveness of AI solutions.

- **Algorithms:** The recipes guiding AI systems. Algorithms are sets of instructions that define how data is processed, analyzed, and used to achieve specific goals.

- **Computing Power:** The engine driving AI. AI algorithms require significant computational resources to process large datasets and train complex models. Advancements in hardware, particularly Graphics Processing Units (GPUs), have accelerated the development of AI solutions.

1.3 The Rise of AI Solutions: Transforming Industries

AI is no longer a futuristic concept - it's actively transforming industries. Here are a few examples of its impact:

- **Manufacturing:** AI is used for predictive maintenance, optimizing production processes, and improving quality control.
- **Finance:** AI-powered fraud detection systems can identify suspicious activity and prevent financial losses. Additionally, AI algorithms can analyze financial markets and recommend investment strategies.
- **Healthcare:** AI is used to analyze medical images for early disease detection, personalize treatment plans, and develop new drugs.

- **Retail:** AI personalizes recommendations for customers, optimizes inventory management, and automates customer service tasks.
- **Transportation:** Self-driving cars and autonomous drones utilize AI for navigation, obstacle detection, and decision-making.

These are just a few examples, and the potential applications of AI continue to expand rapidly. As AI technology matures and becomes more accessible, we can expect even more transformative changes across virtually every sector.

CHAPTER 2

IDENTIFYING BUSINESS NEEDS FOR AI

It's time to bridge the gap between theory and practice. This chapter focuses on identifying business needs that AI can effectively address. By taking a strategic approach, you can leverage AI to solve real-world problems, optimize processes, and achieve significant business value.

2.1 Evaluating Your Business Landscape

Before diving headfirst into AI solutions, a thorough evaluation of your business landscape is crucial. This involves taking a critical look at your current operations, identifying areas for improvement, and understanding your specific goals. Here are some key questions to consider:

- **What are your core business activities and how are they currently performed?** Map out your key processes, identifying bottlenecks and areas with high manual intervention.

- **What are your biggest challenges and pain points?** This could involve inefficiencies, high error rates, limited decision-making capabilities due to lack of data insights, or difficulty in scaling operations. Prioritize challenges that significantly hinder your growth or profitability.
- **What are your long-term business goals?** Are you aiming to increase revenue, improve customer satisfaction, reduce costs, or gain a competitive edge? Understanding your overall vision will guide your AI strategy.
- **What data do you currently collect and how is it used?** Data is the fuel that powers AI. Understanding your existing data resources is essential to determine if you have the necessary foundation for AI implementation. Identify what data is readily available, its quality, and how it's currently being used.

Conducting a Business Process Analysis:

A valuable tool for self-evaluation is a business process analysis. This involves mapping out your key business processes in detail, identifying bottlenecks, and pinpointing areas with high manual intervention or room for error. By visualizing your operations, you can identify potential areas where AI can automate tasks, improve decision-making by analyzing large datasets, or generate valuable insights that were previously hidden.

Here's how to conduct a business process analysis:

1. **Identify key processes:** List the core processes that drive your business, such as order fulfillment, customer service, or marketing campaigns.
2. **Break down each process into steps:** Map out each process step-by-step, including all activities involved, data used, and decision points.
3. **Identify bottlenecks and inefficiencies:** Look for areas with delays, high error rates, or reliance on

manual tasks. These are prime candidates for AI intervention.

4. **Analyze data usage:** Evaluate how data is currently used in each process. Are there opportunities to leverage this data for deeper insights or automated decision-making with AI?

By conducting a thorough business process analysis, you gain a clear understanding of your current operations and can pinpoint areas where AI can deliver the most significant value.

2.2 Defining Problems and Opportunities for AI Integration

Once you have a comprehensive understanding of your business landscape, the next step is to identify specific problems and opportunities where AI can be a game-changer. Here are some key questions to ask:

- **Can AI automate repetitive or time-consuming**

tasks? These could be tasks like data entry, document processing, scheduling appointments, or responding to basic customer inquiries. Freeing up your human workforce for higher-value activities.

- **Can AI improve decision-making by analyzing large datasets?** Imagine AI analyzing customer data to predict churn risk, personalize product recommendations, or dynamically adjust pricing strategies. This data-driven approach can lead to more informed and effective decisions.

- **Can AI generate insights from data that you might be missing?** Large datasets often contain hidden trends and patterns that are difficult for humans to identify. AI algorithms can uncover these patterns, leading to new product ideas, improved customer segmentation, or better understanding of market trends.

Focus on areas where AI can add the most value. Don't be tempted to blindly chase the latest AI trends. Look for areas where AI can address your most pressing challenges, contribute significantly to your business goals, and generate a strong return on investment (ROI).

Examples of AI Applications by Business Function:

Here are some illustrative examples of how AI can be applied across different business functions:

- **Marketing:** AI can personalize advertising campaigns, recommend products to customers, analyze customer sentiment on social media, and even generate creative content.
- **Sales:** AI can identify high-value leads, predict customer needs, automate sales forecasting, and personalize the sales process based on customer data.
- **Operations:** AI can optimize supply chains, predict equipment failures, improve inventory management, and automate scheduling tasks.
- **Finance:** AI can automate financial reporting, detect

fraudulent transactions, manage risk more effectively, and recommend investment strategies based on market analysis.

- **Human Resources:** AI can automate resume screening, personalize employee onboarding, identify potential training needs based on skill gaps, and even analyze employee sentiment to improve company culture.

Think beyond automation. While automation is a valuable capability of AI, it's not the only one. Consider how AI can enhance decision-making by analyzing vast amounts of data, uncover hidden patterns and correlations, and generate new insights to drive strategic advantage.

Here are some additional factors to consider when identifying opportunities for AI integration:

- **Data availability and quality:** Ensure you have the necessary data to train and maintain an AI model effectively. Aim for high-quality, relevant data to achieve optimal results.

- **Scalability of the solution:** Can the AI solution be scaled to accommodate your business growth and changing needs? Consider future-proofing your AI strategy.

- **Ethical considerations:** Be mindful of potential biases in your data and the ethical implications of deploying an AI solution. Ensure transparency and fairness in your AI implementation.

Prioritization is Key:

You'll likely identify multiple opportunities where AI can be beneficial. However, resources are often limited. Here's how to prioritize potential AI projects:

- **Impact on business goals:** Prioritize projects that will have the most significant impact on achieving your overall business objectives.

- **Feasibility and complexity:** Consider the technical feasibility of the project based on your resources and expertise. Start with less complex projects to build your AI implementation experience.

- **Potential return on investment (ROI):** Estimate the potential benefits (increased revenue, cost savings, etc.) and compare them to the costs of implementation. Focus on projects with a clear and measurable ROI.

By systematically evaluating your business landscape, identifying problems and opportunities, and prioritizing projects strategically, you can ensure that your AI initiatives are well-aligned and deliver real value to your organization.

2.3 Aligning AI Solutions with Business Goals

The final step in this stage is to ensure that any AI solution you implement directly aligns with your overall business goals. Here's how:

- **Start with your business objectives.** Don't let

technology dictate your goals. Instead, clearly define your desired outcomes and then explore how AI can help you achieve them. For example, a business goal might be to increase customer retention. AI could then be used to personalize marketing campaigns, predict churn risk, and proactively address customer concerns.

- **Measure success based on business metrics.** Don't simply measure the success of your AI solution based on technical parameters like accuracy. Instead, track how it impacts your key performance indicators (KPIs), such as revenue growth, customer satisfaction, or cost reduction. This ensures that your AI solution is truly driving business value.

- **Develop a clear AI strategy.** Integrate your AI initiatives with your overall business strategy. This will ensure that your AI solutions are aligned with your long-term vision and contribute meaningfully to your success. An AI strategy should outline your goals, target areas, resource allocation, and ethical considerations.

By following these steps, you can effectively identify areas where AI can make a significant contribution to your business. Remember, AI is a powerful tool, but it's your strategic vision and understanding of your specific needs that will unlock its true potential.

CHAPTER 3

Understanding AI Applications Across Industries

Let's explore the diverse landscape of AI applications across various industries. By understanding how AI is transforming different sectors, you can gain valuable insights and inspiration for your own AI strategy.

3.1 AI in Customer Service and Marketing

The customer experience (CX) has become a key differentiator in today's competitive landscape. AI is revolutionizing how businesses interact with their customers, making it more personalized, efficient, and effective. Here are some prominent applications:

- **Chatbots and Virtual Assistants:** AI-powered chatbots provide 24/7 customer support, answer frequently asked questions, and can even resolve simple customer issues. This frees up human agents to handle more complex inquiries and builds customer satisfaction through faster resolution times.

- **Recommendation Engines:** AI algorithms analyze customer data, such as past purchases, browsing history, and demographics, to recommend products, services, or content that aligns with their individual preferences. This personalizes the shopping experience and increases conversion rates.

- **Sentiment Analysis:** AI can analyze customer feedback on social media, reviews, and surveys to understand customer sentiment towards your brand, products, or services. This allows businesses to identify areas for improvement, address customer concerns promptly, and enhance overall brand reputation.

- **Marketing Automation:** AI automates repetitive tasks in marketing campaigns, such as email marketing, social media scheduling, and ad targeting. It can also personalize marketing messages based on customer demographics, behavior, and interests, leading to more targeted and impactful campaigns.

Benefits of AI in Customer Service and Marketing:

- Improved customer satisfaction through faster response times, personalized interactions, and proactive problem-solving.
- Increased sales and revenue through targeted marketing campaigns and personalized recommendations.
- Reduced operational costs by automating routine tasks and leveraging AI for more efficient customer service.
- Gain valuable customer insights from data analysis, allowing for better product development and marketing strategies.

3.2 AI in Manufacturing and Supply Chain Management

AI is transforming the manufacturing sector by optimizing processes, improving efficiency, and minimizing waste. Here are some notable applications:

- **Predictive Maintenance:** AI algorithms analyze sensor data from equipment to predict potential failures before they occur. This allows for proactive maintenance, reducing downtime, production losses, and associated costs.
- **Quality Control:** AI-powered vision systems can inspect products for defects with high accuracy and speed, ensuring consistent quality throughout the production line. This minimizes human error and reduces the need for manual inspections.
- **Demand Forecasting:** AI can analyze historical sales data, market trends, and social media sentiment to predict future demand for products. This allows for better inventory management, production planning, and reduces the risk of stockouts or overstocking.

- **Supply Chain Optimization:** AI can optimize logistics by analyzing real-time data on traffic, weather, and inventory levels. This allows for efficient routing of shipments, reduces transportation costs, and ensures on-time delivery.

Benefits of AI in Manufacturing and Supply Chain Management:

- Increased production efficiency through predictive maintenance, optimized processes, and reduced downtime.
- Improved product quality with automated defect detection and consistent quality control.
- Reduced costs through optimized inventory management, demand forecasting, and efficient logistics.
- Enhanced supply chain visibility and control with real-time data analysis.

3.3 AI in Healthcare and Life Sciences

AI is making significant advancements in healthcare, from improving diagnostic accuracy to accelerating drug discovery. Here are some impactful applications:

- **Medical Imaging Analysis:** AI algorithms can analyze medical images like X-rays, CT scans, and MRIs to detect diseases at an early stage, improve diagnosis accuracy, and lead to better treatment outcomes. This can be particularly valuable in areas like cancer detection.
- **Personalized Medicine:** AI can analyze a patient's genetic information and medical history to predict their response to specific treatments. This allows for personalized healthcare plans that are tailored to the individual patient, leading to improved treatment efficacy and reduced side effects.
- **Drug Discovery and Development:** AI can analyze vast amounts of data on molecules and biological processes to identify potential drug candidates. This significantly accelerates the drug discovery process

and can lead to the development of new treatments for various diseases.

- **Robotic Surgery:** AI-powered surgical robots assist surgeons with increased precision and minimal invasiveness, leading to improved patient outcomes and faster recovery times. Additionally, AI can analyze data during surgery to provide real-time insights and guidance to surgeons.

Benefits of AI in Healthcare and Life Sciences:

- Improved diagnostic accuracy and early disease detection through medical image analysis.
- Personalized medicine for better treatment efficacy and reduced side effects.
- Faster drug discovery and development with AI-powered analysis of vast datasets.
- Enhanced surgical precision and improved patient outcomes with robotic surgery and AI assistance.

These are just a few examples, and the potential

applications of AI in healthcare and life sciences continue to expand rapidly. AI is also being used for tasks like:

- **Administrative tasks:** Automating tasks like appointment scheduling, claims processing, and patient record management, freeing up healthcare professionals to focus on patient care.

- **Epidemic prediction and prevention:** AI can analyze data on disease outbreaks, travel patterns, and social media to predict and prevent the spread of epidemics.

- **Drug development and clinical trials:** AI can optimize the design of clinical trials, analyze patient data to identify potential safety concerns, and accelerate the development of new drugs.

The Future of AI in Healthcare:

As AI technology continues to evolve, we can expect even more transformative applications in healthcare. Here are some potential areas of future development:

- **AI-powered diagnostics:** AI could analyze a wider range of data points, including a patient's voice, gait, and even facial expressions, to provide more comprehensive and accurate diagnoses.
- **Virtual assistants for patients:** AI-powered virtual assistants could provide patients with personalized health information, medication reminders, and even basic mental health support.
- **AI-driven drug discovery:** AI could play an even greater role in drug discovery, leading to the development of personalized therapies and more effective treatments for complex diseases.

Ethical Considerations in Healthcare AI

While the potential benefits of AI in healthcare are vast, there are also ethical considerations that need to be addressed. These include:

- **Bias in AI algorithms:** AI algorithms trained on

biased data can perpetuate those biases in healthcare decisions. It's crucial to ensure fairness and inclusivity in AI development and deployment.

- **Data privacy and security:** Protecting patient data privacy is paramount when using AI in healthcare. Robust security measures are essential to prevent data breaches and misuse of sensitive information.

- **Transparency and explainability:** Healthcare professionals and patients need to understand how AI-powered decisions are made. Explainable AI models are crucial to ensure trust and transparency in healthcare applications.

By addressing these ethical challenges, AI can be a powerful tool for improving healthcare outcomes and ensuring equitable access to quality care for everyone.

3.4 AI in Other Industries

The transformative potential of AI extends far beyond the industries mentioned above. Here are some additional examples:

- **Finance:** AI is used for fraud detection, risk management, personalized financial advice, and algorithmic trading.
- **Law:** AI can analyze legal documents, predict the outcome of lawsuits, and assist with legal research.
- **Media and Entertainment:** AI is used for content creation, recommendation engines for personalized entertainment experiences, and targeted advertising.
- **Transportation:** AI is being used for autonomous vehicles, traffic management optimization, and predictive maintenance of transportation infrastructure.

As AI technology continues to develop and become more accessible, we can expect even broader adoption and innovation across all sectors.

The Road Ahead

With a foundational understanding of AI applications

across industries, the next chapters will delve deeper into the technical aspects of AI implementation. We'll explore how to choose the right AI approach for your specific needs, discuss the process of building and training AI models, and address critical considerations like data preparation and model deployment. We'll also explore the future trajectory of AI and its potential impact on society and the workforce.

CHAPTER 4

PLANNING AND DESIGN FOR AI IMPLEMENTATION

Having identified areas where AI can truly benefit your business, it's time to delve into the planning and design phases of implementing an AI solution.

4.1 Defining Project Scope and Success Metrics

Before diving headfirst into development, a well-defined project scope is crucial. This involves outlining the specific problem your AI solution will address, the desired outcomes, and the resources required. Here are some key questions to consider:

- **What specific goals do you want your AI solution to achieve?** Be clear and measurable in your objectives. For example, are you aiming to improve customer satisfaction by 10%, increase sales by 5%, or reduce production costs by 2%? Having quantifiable goals allows you to track progress and measure success.

- **Who are the stakeholders involved in this project?** Identify key decision-makers, end-users (those who will interact with the AI solution), and any other individuals who will be impacted by the AI implementation. Involving stakeholders throughout the process promotes buy-in and ensures the solution aligns with their needs.

- **What are the technical and budgetary constraints?** AI projects can be resource-intensive. Be realistic about your resources and capabilities. Consider factors like available hardware, software, and the expertise of your team.

- **What is the timeline for implementation?** Set realistic timelines for data preparation, model building, training, testing, and deployment. Factor in potential delays and allow time for iteration and refinement.

Defining Success Metrics

Measuring the success of your AI solution is paramount. Define key performance indicators (KPIs) that align with your project goals. These metrics will allow you to track progress, evaluate the effectiveness of your AI solution, and identify areas for improvement. Examples of KPIs for AI projects might include:

- **Accuracy**: Measures how well the AI model performs its intended task. This could be the percentage of correctly classified emails in sentiment analysis or the accuracy of product recommendations in a recommender system.
- **Efficiency**: Tracks how much time and resources are saved through AI automation. For instance, measure the reduction in processing time for loan applications with an AI-powered underwriting system.
- **Cost reduction**: Quantifies the financial savings generated by the AI solution. This could involve cost savings from reduced errors, improved inventory

management, or optimized logistics.

- **Customer satisfaction**: Assesses how AI implementation has improved the customer experience. Track metrics like customer satisfaction surveys, response times, or resolution rates for customer inquiries.

By clearly defining your project scope, identifying stakeholders, setting realistic timelines, and establishing relevant KPIs, you lay the groundwork for a successful AI implementation.

4.2 Choosing the Right AI Approach (Machine Learning, Deep Learning etc.)

There's no one-size-fits-all approach to AI. The best choice depends on your specific problem and data characteristics. Here's an overview of some common AI approaches:

- **Machine Learning (ML):** This broad field encompasses various techniques that allow computers to learn from data without explicit programming. Subfields like decision trees, support vector machines, and k-nearest neighbors offer diverse solutions for tasks like classification, regression, and clustering. ML algorithms excel at identifying patterns and making predictions from structured data.

- **Deep Learning:** A subset of ML particularly powerful for tasks involving complex data like images, text, or audio. Deep learning utilizes artificial neural networks with multiple layers, enabling them to learn intricate patterns from vast datasets. This makes deep learning well-suited for tasks like image recognition, natural language processing, and complex pattern analysis.

- **Natural Language Processing (NLP):** Enables computers to understand and process human language. This is crucial for tasks like chatbots, sentiment analysis, text summarization, and machine translation. NLP techniques involve analyzing text data, identifying keywords, and understanding the relationships between words to extract meaning.

- **Computer Vision:** Allows machines to analyze and interpret visual information from images or videos. This has applications in areas like object recognition, facial recognition, medical image analysis, and autonomous vehicle navigation. Computer vision algorithms extract features from images and videos, allowing for classification, object detection, and scene understanding.

Understanding the trade-offs: Each approach has its own strengths and weaknesses. Consider factors like:

- **Data availability:** Some approaches, like deep learning, require vast amounts of data for training. Ensure you have sufficient data to effectively train your chosen AI model.
- **Computational power required:** Deep learning models can be computationally expensive to train. Consider your available computing resources and the

feasibility of training complex models.

- **Interpretability:** Some models are more interpretable than others. If understanding how the AI model arrives at its decisions is crucial for your project (e.g., ensuring fairness in loan approvals), consider interpretable ML models like decision trees.
- **Project complexity:** For simpler tasks with well-defined patterns, traditional machine learning techniques might suffice. For complex tasks involving unstructured data like images or text, deep learning approaches may be more suitable.

Additional Considerations:

- **Hybrid approaches:** Combining different AI techniques can be advantageous in some cases. For example, you might use NLP to pre-process text data before feeding it into a deep learning model for sentiment analysis.
- **Explainable AI (XAI):** As interpretability becomes increasingly important, XAI techniques are being

developed to help us understand how AI models make decisions. This is crucial for building trust and ensuring fairness in AI applications.

By carefully considering these factors and the specific needs of your project, you can select the most appropriate AI approach for your AI solution.

4.3 Data Acquisition and Preparation for AI Models

Data is the lifeblood of any AI project. The quality and quantity of data significantly impact the performance and effectiveness of your AI solution. Here's what you need to consider:

- **Data Acquisition:** Identify what data you need for your AI model. Depending on your application, this might involve internal data sources, publicly available datasets, or collecting new data through surveys or sensors.
- **Data Cleaning and Preprocessing:** Raw data often

contains inconsistencies, missing values, and errors. These need to be addressed through data cleaning techniques before feeding the data into your AI model. This might involve handling missing values, correcting inconsistencies, and formatting the data appropriately for your chosen AI approach.

- **Data Labeling:** Certain AI approaches, particularly supervised learning, require labeled data. This involves annotating data points with the desired outcome, allowing the model to learn the relationship between input and output. For example, in image recognition, you might label images with the objects they contain.

- **Data Security and Governance:** Ensure your data practices comply with relevant regulations and protect sensitive information. Implement robust security measures to prevent data breaches and ensure responsible data handling throughout the AI development lifecycle.

Data is a valuable asset. Invest time and resources into data acquisition, cleaning, and preparation. High-quality data is essential for training effective AI models that deliver real value.

CHAPTER 5

BUILDING AND TRAINING AI MODELS

This chapter will guide you through the essential steps involved in bringing your AI solution to life.

5.1 Selecting AI Tools and Platforms

The landscape of AI tools and platforms is constantly evolving, offering a wide range of options for building and training your models. Here are some key factors to consider when selecting the right tools:

- **Technical Expertise:** Consider your team's skills and experience with AI development tools. Some platforms are designed for users with advanced programming knowledge, while others offer more user-friendly interfaces for beginners.
- **Project Requirements:** The complexity of your

project will influence your choice of tools. For simpler tasks, low-code or no-code platforms might be sufficient. Complex projects requiring deep learning might necessitate using libraries like TensorFlow or PyTorch.

- **Scalability:** Consider the potential growth of your AI solution. Choose tools that can scale to handle larger datasets and increased processing demands as your project matures.

- **Integration Capabilities:** Ensure the chosen tools integrate seamlessly with your existing infrastructure and data sources. This will streamline the development process and facilitate deployment of your AI solution.

Here's an overview of some popular AI development tools and platforms:

- **Cloud-based platforms:** Services like Google Cloud AI Platform, Amazon SageMaker, and Microsoft Azure Machine Learning offer comprehensive tool sets for building, training, and deploying AI models. They provide pre-built components, managed infrastructure, and scalability for large-scale projects.

- **Open-source libraries:** Libraries like TensorFlow, PyTorch, and scikit-learn provide powerful building blocks for custom AI development. These offer greater flexibility and control, but require more programming expertise.
- **Low-code/no-code platforms:** These platforms offer user-friendly interfaces that allow users with limited coding experience to build and train simple AI models. They typically involve drag-and-drop functionality and pre-built templates, making AI development more accessible.

Remember, the best tool is the one that best suits your specific needs and skillset. Don't be afraid to experiment and explore different options before making a decision.

5.2 Training Data Management and Optimization

The quality of your training data significantly impacts the performance of your AI model. Here's how to ensure you're using your data effectively:

- **Data Augmentation:** Techniques like flipping images, adding noise, or rotating text can artificially increase the size and diversity of your training data. This helps the model generalize better and perform well on unseen data.

- **Active Learning:** This approach prioritizes labeling the most informative data points for the model's learning process. This can be particularly helpful when dealing with limited labeled data.

- **Feature Engineering:** The process of transforming raw data into features that are more meaningful and usable for the AI model. This can involve feature selection, dimensionality reduction, and creating new features based on existing data.

Data optimization is crucial. By implementing these techniques, you can ensure your model learns from the right data and achieves optimal performance.

5.3 Model Training, Evaluation, and Refinement

Now it's time to train your AI model! Here's a breakdown of the key steps:

- **Model Selection:** Based on your chosen AI approach (e.g., Machine Learning, Deep Learning), select the appropriate model architecture for your project. Different model architectures have varying strengths and weaknesses for specific tasks.
- **Model Training:** The model learns from the training data, identifying patterns and relationships. This process typically involves iterative training cycles, where the model is exposed to the data, makes predictions, and adjusts its internal parameters to improve its accuracy.
- **Model Evaluation:** Once training is complete,

evaluate the model's performance on a separate hold-out dataset that wasn't used for training. This unbiased evaluation provides a more accurate picture of how well the model will perform in real-world scenarios. Common evaluation metrics include accuracy, precision, recall, and F1-score.

- **Model Refinement:** Based on the evaluation results, you may need to refine your model. This could involve adjusting hyperparameters (tuning knobs of the model), gathering more data, or even trying a different model architecture.

Model training is an iterative process. Be prepared to experiment, refine, and improve your model until it meets your performance expectations.

Additional Considerations:

- **Overfitting:** This occurs when the model memorizes the training data too well and performs poorly on unseen data. Techniques like using a hold-out set for evaluation and regularization techniques can help prevent overfitting.

- **Underfitting:** This happens when the model is too simple and fails to capture the underlying patterns in the data, resulting in poor performance on both training and testing data. Choosing a more complex model architecture or gathering more data can address underfitting.

- **Bias-variance trade-off:** There's a trade-off between bias (the model's tendency to underfit) and variance (the model's tendency to overfit). Regularization techniques can help achieve a balance between these two factors.

By understanding these concepts and employing appropriate techniques, you can effectively train and evaluate your AI model, ensuring it generalizes well and delivers robust performance on unseen data.

CHAPTER 6

INTEGRATING AI SOLUTIONS INTO EXISTING SYSTEMS

This chapter explores the crucial steps involved in integrating your AI solution into your existing systems and ensuring its seamless operation.

6.1 Data Pipelines and Infrastructure Development

For your AI model to function effectively in the real world, it needs a steady stream of data. Here's what you need to consider:

- **Data Pipelines:** Develop a reliable data pipeline that continuously extracts data from your source systems, cleans and preprocesses it, and feeds it to your AI model in real-time or at regular intervals. This ensures the model has access to the latest information for accurate predictions or decision-making.

- **Infrastructure Development:** Depending on the complexity of your AI model, you might need to invest in additional computing infrastructure. Consider cloud-based solutions or upgrading your on-premises hardware to handle the processing demands of your AI application.

- **Model Management:** Establish a robust system for managing your AI model throughout its lifecycle. This includes version control, monitoring performance, and scheduling retraining when necessary.

Investing in a well-designed data pipeline and infrastructure is crucial. It ensures your AI model has the resources it needs to operate effectively and deliver consistent value.

6.2 User Interface and User Experience Design for AI Integration

How will users interact with your AI solution? Here's how to design a user experience that promotes adoption and maximizes benefits:

- **User Interface (UI) Design:** Create an intuitive and user-friendly interface that allows users to interact with your AI solution easily. Consider factors like user roles, information needs, and the overall workflow of your application.

- **User Experience (UX) Design:** Focus on designing a positive experience for users interacting with your AI solution. This means providing clear instructions, transparent explanations of AI recommendations, and mechanisms for user feedback.

- **Explainable AI (XAI):** If interpretability is crucial for your project, consider incorporating XAI techniques. This allows users to understand how the AI model arrives at its decisions, fostering trust and confidence in the technology.

A well-designed user interface and user experience are

critical for successful AI adoption. Make sure your AI solution is easy to use, informative, and empowers users to leverage its capabilities effectively.

6.3 Change Management and User Adoption Strategies

Integrating AI into your organization can bring significant changes to workflows and processes. Here's how to ensure a smooth transition and maximize user adoption:

- **Change Management Strategy:** Develop a comprehensive change management strategy to address potential challenges and guide users through the transition to an AI-powered environment. This may involve training programs, communication plans, and addressing user concerns.
- **User Adoption Strategies:** Encourage user buy-in and active engagement with your AI solution. This could involve showcasing success stories, highlighting the benefits of AI for users, and providing ongoing support and training.

- **Iterative Development:** Be prepared to iterate on your AI solution based on user feedback. Continuously gather feedback, identify areas for improvement, and refine your model and user experience over time.

Successful AI implementation requires more than just technology. Focus on managing change effectively, fostering user adoption, and continuously improving your AI solution based on user experience.

6.4 Monitoring and Maintaining AI Models

Deploying your AI model is not the finish line. Here's how to ensure it continues to perform well over time:

- **Model Monitoring:** Continuously monitor the performance of your AI model in production. Track key metrics like accuracy, bias, and drift (changes in the data distribution over time that can impact model performance).

- **Model Retraining:** As new data becomes available or the underlying data distribution changes, retrain your model periodically to maintain its accuracy and effectiveness. This ensures your AI solution adapts to changing circumstances and delivers consistent value.

- **Data Governance and Security:** Maintain robust data governance practices and security measures to protect sensitive data throughout the AI lifecycle. This includes data privacy compliance, access controls, and data security protocols.

By actively monitoring, maintaining, and retraining your AI model, you ensure it remains relevant, reliable, and continues to deliver the benefits you envisioned.

CHAPTER 7

TESTING AND DEPLOYMENT OF AI SOLUTIONS

Let's explore crucial steps for ensuring a successful launch, including rigorous testing, security considerations, ethical implications, and ongoing monitoring processes.

7.1 Performance Testing and Benchmarking

Before unleashing your AI solution on the real world, thorough testing is paramount. Here's what you need to consider:

- **Performance Testing:** Evaluate the performance of your AI solution under various load conditions. This ensures it can handle real-world usage patterns without performance degradation or delays. Tools like load testing frameworks can simulate high traffic scenarios and identify potential bottlenecks.

- **Functional Testing:** Verify that the AI solution functions as intended and delivers the expected results. This involves testing different functionalities, edge cases, and user interactions to ensure everything works seamlessly.
- **Benchmarking:** Compare the performance of your AI model against other models or existing solutions for the same task. This provides a valuable reference point and helps identify areas for further improvement.

Rigorous testing builds confidence. By identifying and addressing performance issues before deployment, you ensure your AI solution delivers a smooth and reliable user experience.

7.2 Security Considerations and Ethical Implications of AI

AI, like any technology, comes with its own set of security and ethical considerations:

- **Security Threats:** AI systems can be vulnerable to various security threats, such as adversarial attacks where malicious actors manipulate data to trick the model into making false predictions. Implementing robust security measures like data encryption and access controls is crucial.
- **Bias and Fairness:** AI models can perpetuate biases present in the data they are trained on. This can lead to discriminatory outcomes. It's crucial to identify and mitigate potential biases in your data and model development process.
- **Explainability and Transparency:** Understanding how AI models arrive at their decisions is essential, especially in high-stakes scenarios. Techniques like Explainable AI (XAI) can help build trust and transparency in your AI solution.
- **Privacy Concerns:** AI applications often involve collecting and processing sensitive data. Ensure you have proper data governance practices in place to protect user privacy and comply with relevant

regulations.

Addressing security and ethical considerations is essential. By proactively mitigating risks and being transparent about how your AI solution works, you build trust and ensure responsible AI development and deployment.

7.3 Deployment Strategies and Monitoring Processes

Now it's time to launch your AI solution! Here's how to ensure a smooth deployment and ongoing monitoring:

- **Deployment Strategies:** Choose the appropriate deployment strategy for your needs. This could involve on-premises deployment, cloud deployment, or a hybrid approach. Consider factors like scalability, security, and ongoing maintenance requirements.
- **A/B Testing:** Consider using A/B testing to compare the performance of your AI solution with the

existing system. This allows you to measure the impact of AI and gradually roll out the solution to a wider audience.

- **Monitoring and Logging:** Establish robust monitoring processes to track the performance of your AI solution in production. This includes monitoring key metrics, identifying errors, and logging data for future analysis and improvement.

Deployment is not a one-time event. Continuously monitor your AI solution, identify areas for optimization, and iterate based on user feedback and real-world data. This ensures your AI solution remains effective and delivers ongoing value.

CHAPTER 8

EVALUATING AND MAINTAINING AI SYSTEMS

Having deployed your AI solution, the journey doesn't end there. Just like any complex system, effective AI requires ongoing evaluation, maintenance, and improvement.

8.1 Monitoring AI Performance and Model Drift

Just because your AI model performed well during testing doesn't guarantee its continued effectiveness in the real world. Here's why continuous monitoring is crucial:

- **Performance Metrics:** Track key performance indicators (KPIs) aligned with your project goals. This could include accuracy, precision, recall, or business-specific metrics like customer satisfaction or cost reduction. Monitor these metrics over time to identify any performance degradation.

- **Model Drift:** Real-world data can change over time, causing a phenomenon known as model drift. This occurs when the underlying distribution of the data your model was trained on deviates from the data it encounters in production. Monitoring for drift helps identify when your model's predictions become unreliable and require retraining.

- **Alerting and Escalation:** Establish clear thresholds for your KPIs and model drift metrics. Set up alerts to notify you when these thresholds are crossed, allowing for prompt intervention and potential model retraining.

Proactive monitoring is key. By continuously tracking performance and identifying potential issues early on, you can maintain the effectiveness and reliability of your AI solution.

8.2 Continuous Improvement and Model Retraining

The world around us is constantly evolving, and your AI

solution needs to adapt as well. Here's how to ensure continuous improvement:

- **Data Feedback Loops:** Establish feedback loops that incorporate new data into your AI model. This could involve user feedback mechanisms, real-time data streams, or scheduled retraining cycles based on new data availability.
- **Model Retraining:** Periodically retrain your AI model with fresh data to account for changes in the real world and mitigate model drift. This ensures your model remains accurate and delivers optimal performance.
- **A/B Testing for Improvements:** Consider using A/B testing to evaluate different versions of your AI model. This allows you to compare the performance of a newly trained model against the deployed version and identify improvements before a full rollout.

Continuous improvement is an ongoing process. By

incorporating new data, retraining your model, and iteratively testing enhancements, you ensure your AI solution stays relevant and delivers increasing value over time.

8.3 Explainability and Transparency in AI Decisions

As AI becomes more integrated into our lives, understanding how these models arrive at decisions is crucial. Here's why explainability and transparency matter:

- **Building Trust:** When users understand the reasoning behind AI recommendations, it fosters trust and confidence in the technology. Techniques like Explainable AI (XAI) can make AI decision-making processes more transparent.
- **Debugging and Improvement:** Explainability can help identify biases or errors in your AI model. By understanding how the model arrived at a particular decision, you can diagnose issues and improve its performance.

- **Regulatory Compliance:** Certain regulations might require explainability for AI used in high-stakes scenarios. Being able to explain how your AI model functions is essential for compliance purposes.

Explainability is no longer a luxury, but a necessity. By incorporating XAI techniques and promoting transparency in your AI development process, you build trust, ensure responsible AI practices, and comply with evolving regulations.

CHAPTER 9

THE FUTURE OF AI: TRENDS AND ADVANCEMENTS

The world of AI is progressing at an astounding pace. This chapter explores the exciting frontiers of AI, delving into emerging technologies, their potential applications, and the broader societal implications of AI's growing influence.

9.1 Emerging AI Technologies and Applications

AI is rapidly evolving, with new advancements constantly emerging. Here are some key trends shaping the future of AI:

- **Explainable AI (XAI):** As discussed previously, XAI techniques are becoming increasingly crucial for building trust and transparency in AI decision-making. Advancements in XAI will allow us to better understand how AI models arrive at their conclusions.

- **Generative AI:** This subfield focuses on models that can generate entirely new content, like realistic images, creative text formats, or even musical pieces. Generative AI holds immense potential for various creative and artistic applications.

- **Reinforcement Learning:** This approach involves training AI models through trial and error, allowing them to learn by interacting with an environment and receiving rewards for desired behaviors. Reinforcement learning has applications in robotics, game playing, and complex control systems.

- **Neuromorphic Computing:** This emerging field aims to develop computer hardware inspired by the human brain. Neuromorphic chips could potentially offer significant advantages in terms of processing power and efficiency for specific AI tasks.

These advancements are just the tip of the iceberg. The future of AI holds the potential for groundbreaking advancements in various domains:

- **Healthcare:** AI can revolutionize medical diagnosis, treatment planning, and drug discovery by analyzing vast amounts of medical data and identifying patterns invisible to human experts.
- **Transportation:** Autonomous vehicles powered by AI have the potential to transform our transportation systems, improving safety and efficiency.
- **Manufacturing:** AI-powered robots and intelligent automation can streamline production processes, optimize resource allocation, and improve quality control in manufacturing.
- **Customer Service:** AI-powered chatbots and virtual assistants can provide personalized customer service experiences, answer questions, and resolve issues efficiently.

The applications of AI are vast and continuously expanding, promising to reshape various aspects of our lives.

9.2 The Impact of AI on Jobs and the Workforce

The rise of AI raises questions about its impact on jobs and the future of work. Here's a closer look:

- **Job Automation:** AI automation may replace some routine tasks currently performed by humans. However, AI is also creating new job opportunities in fields like AI development, data science, and cybersecurity.

- **Upskilling and Reskilling:** The workforce will need to adapt to the changing landscape. Upskilling and reskilling initiatives will be crucial to equip workers with the skills necessary to thrive in an AI-powered future.

- **Human-AI Collaboration:** The future of work likely involves humans and AI collaborating effectively. AI can handle repetitive tasks, freeing up human workers to focus on creativity, problem-solving, and higher-order cognitive skills.

AI is a tool, and like any tool, its impact depends on how we use it. By proactively preparing our workforce and fostering human-AI collaboration, we can harness the potential of AI to create a more efficient, productive, and prosperous future for all.

9.3 Responsible AI Development and Governance

As AI becomes more powerful, ethical considerations and responsible development practices are paramount:

- **Bias in AI:** AI models can perpetuate biases present in the data they are trained on. It's crucial to develop and deploy AI systems that are fair, unbiased, and inclusive.
- **Privacy and Security:** AI applications often involve collecting and processing sensitive data. Robust data governance practices and security measures are essential to protect privacy and prevent misuse of data.
- **Transparency and Explainability:** Users deserve to

understand how AI systems work and the reasoning behind their decisions. Explainable AI techniques and transparent development processes are crucial for building trust in AI.

- **Algorithmic Accountability:** As AI plays an increasingly significant role in decision-making, establishing frameworks for algorithmic accountability is critical. This ensures fairness, reduces potential harm, and promotes responsible AI development.

Addressing these considerations is crucial. By developing and deploying AI responsibly, we can ensure it benefits society as a whole and promotes positive change.

CHAPTER 10

Conclusion: A Roadmap to AI Success

Throughout this book, we've explored the fundamentals of AI, delved into the process of building and deploying AI solutions, and examined the potential impact of AI on our world. Now, it's time to solidify your learnings and chart your own roadmap to AI success.

10.1 Key Takeaways for Implementing AI Solutions

Here are some key takeaways to keep in mind as you embark on your AI implementation journey:

- **Start with a clear business need:** Don't jump into AI for the sake of it. Identify a specific problem or opportunity where AI can deliver tangible value.
- **Choose the right approach:** Understand the different AI techniques available and select the

approach best suited for your specific project and data.

- **Data is king:** High-quality, well-prepared data is essential for building effective AI models. Invest time and resources in data acquisition, cleaning, and labeling.

- **Focus on interpretability:** Consider the importance of explainability, especially for high-stakes applications. Explore XAI techniques to build trust and transparency in your AI solutions.

- **Iterate and improve:** Building and deploying AI is an iterative process. Continuously monitor performance, gather feedback, and refine your model for optimal results.

- **Embrace responsible AI:** Develop and deploy AI solutions that are fair, unbiased, and secure. Prioritize data privacy, algorithmic accountability, and ethical considerations throughout the AI lifecycle.

By following these principles, you can increase your chances of successfully implementing AI and achieving your desired outcomes.

10.2 Building an AI-Ready Organization

Successfully integrating AI into your organization requires more than just technology. Here's how to cultivate an AI-ready culture:

- **Leadership buy-in:** Ensure strong leadership support for AI initiatives. Leaders need to champion AI adoption and create a clear vision for its role within the organization.
- **Upskilling and reskilling:** Invest in training programs to equip your workforce with the skills needed to understand and work effectively with AI systems.
- **Change management strategy:** Develop a comprehensive change management strategy to address potential challenges and guide employees

through the transition to an AI-powered environment.

- **Culture of innovation:** Foster a culture of innovation and experimentation. Encourage exploration, learning from failures, and continuous improvement.
- **Focus on human-AI collaboration:** AI is not here to replace humans, but to augment our capabilities. Focus on building strong human-AI partnerships for optimal results.

Creating an AI-ready organization empowers your workforce to leverage AI for positive change and unlock new opportunities.

10.3 The Journey Continues: A Look Ahead

The field of AI is constantly evolving, offering exciting possibilities for the future. Here's a glimpse of what lies ahead:

- **Advancements in AI capabilities:** Expect to see continuous advancements in areas like Explainable AI, generative models, and neuromorphic computing, further expanding the potential applications of AI.
- **The rise of AI ethics:** As AI becomes more integrated into society, discussions surrounding AI ethics, responsible development, and algorithmic accountability will continue to gain prominence.
- **Focus on human-AI collaboration:** The future of work will likely involve seamless collaboration between humans and AI, leveraging the strengths of both to achieve optimal results.

The possibilities with AI are vast. Embrace the journey of continuous learning and exploration. Stay curious, keep up with the latest advancements, and actively participate in shaping the future of AI.

This book has provided a foundational understanding of AI. However, the journey doesn't end here. The world of AI is brimming with potential, and the future is waiting to be shaped. Leverage the knowledge you've gained, embrace continuous learning, and actively contribute to building a responsible and beneficial future powered by AI.

ABOUT THE AUTHOR

Writer's Bio:

Benjamin Evans, a respected figure in the tech world, is known for his insightful commentary and analysis. With a strong educational background likely in fields such as computer science, engineering, or business, he brings a depth of knowledge to his discussions on emerging technologies and industry trends. Evans' knack for simplifying complex concepts, coupled with his innate curiosity and passion for innovation, has established him as a go-to source for understanding the dynamics of the digital landscape. Through articles, speeches, and social media, he shares his expertise and offers valuable insights into the impact of technology on society.

www.ingramcontent.com/pod-product-compliance
Lightning Source LLC
Chambersburg PA
CBHW050234230526
45470CB00005B/1947